DESIGN
STYLES

Unleash your creativity and update
every room in an instant

DESIGN
STYLES

p

This is a Parragon Book
First printed in 2002

Parragon
Queen Street House
4 Queen Street
Bath BA1 1HE
United Kingdom

Created and produced by The Bridgewater Book Company Ltd, Lewes, East Sussex

Creative Director Steve Knowlden
Art Director Johnny Pau
Editorial Director Fiona Biggs
Senior Editor Mark Truman
Photographers Steve Gorton, Alistair Hughes

ISBN: 0-75256-995-3

Printed in China

Contents

Introduction   6

Painter's Palette   8

Floors & Walls   22

Window Ways   34

Furniture Facelifts   46

What's in Store?   58

Going Soft   70

Little Details   82

Index   94

Introduction

From stencilling and painting to making cupboards and soft furnishings, *Design Styles* offers a wealth of inspiring ideas to liven up your home. Whether you like small design details that can bring a touch of colour and class and have a big impact on your living environment or you want to revamp a room completely, there are projects here to suit you. Whatever your level of expertise, you can quickly and easily add colour and style to your home.

ABOVE **A plain lamp base can be modified to provide an attractive detail in a room's decorative scheme or even to form the keynote of a room's style. Here the seaside is evoked through the use of shells and a wet sand look applied to the base of a table lamp.**

If you want to liven up your lounge or give your bedroom decor a boost, then you need look no further than this book. There is a whole raft of simple step-by-step projects aimed at transforming your living space.

Nothing transforms an entire room quite like paint. Paint techniques that are easy to learn but bring impressive results are featured in Painter's Palette (pages 8–21). Projects here include inspiring and evocative ideas from Morocco, Africa and the Mediterranean. There is also guidance on different paint techniques and styles. You can try painting checks or blocks of colour or experiment with stencilling.

Stencilling is not just confined to wall projects, however. In Floors & Walls (pages 22–33) we show you how to stencil a floor border. There are also projects on laying a floating wooden floor and ideas for making walls more interesting with tongue-and-groove panelling or cane wall panels.

The need to screen out light and noise from a room need not mean that curtains and blinds have to be purely functional. In Window Ways (pages 34–45) we show how to make tab-head curtains and muslin no-sew curtains that are in themselves attractive features.

Revamping old furniture is a satisfying way of cheering up tired old items and saving money. In

Furniture Facelifts (pages 46–57) you will discover how to transform tables, chairs and headboards using a variety of materials, including paint, strong utility fabric and even mosaic tiles.

The search for sufficient storage space is a constant bugbear in the modern home. In What's in Store? (pages 58–69) we look at ways of increasing storage space in attractive and stylish ways. Whether you're considering extra shelving, making a small cupboard or simply wanting to transform the look of your storage system, there's a project idea here for you.

Going Soft (pages 70–81) includes a raft of soft furnishings projects, from floor cushions to quilts, that will not only bring warmth and comfort but also provide accent colours and focal points to your living space.

It's the smallest design details in a house that really turn it into a home, as Little Details (pages 82–93) will demonstrate!

ABOVE **By simply removing cupboard doors from a plain base unit and using willow baskets on the shelves as pull-out drawers, you can give a room a completely new country look.**

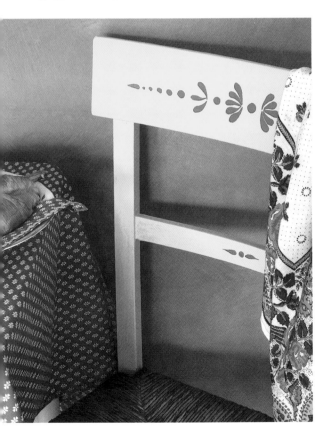

LEFT **Revamping old furniture is not only great fun, it saves money and can help to give your home a different feeling altogether. This table and chair have been renovated in a lively Provençal style to evoke the feeling of rural France.**

Painter's Palette

Choosing the correct colour scheme for your home is one of the most important decisions you will have to make about home decoration because it has a major impact on how you feel about your living space. You might find inspiration in the colour schemes and design ideas included here from around the world, whether it's the rusty reds, earthy browns and yellow ochres of the African landscape or the cool, chalky colours of Mediterranean homes.

Painting styles can be lively and fun, too. Consider the powerful potential of stencils – a very simple but effective means of transforming a room. Colour-blocking can provide a very dramatic visual feature in a lounge or hallway, and why not consider an appealing gingham wall to brighten up a nursery?

YOU WILL NEED:

- POWDER BLUE PAINT
  FOR BACKGROUND
- SAMPLE POTS OF
  TWO PINKS
- SAMPLE POT OF GREEN
- STENCIL MATERIAL
  (MYLAR OR STENCIL
  CARD IF YOU PREFER),
  OR BUY A READY-CUT
  ROSE STENCIL
- SPRAYMOUNT
- SCALPEL OR CRAFT
  KNIFE
- 3 STENCIL BRUSHES
- 3 WHITE SAUCERS
- PLUMB LINE
- SQUARE OF CARD
  (TO MARK DISTANCE
  BETWEEN MOTIFS).
  THE SIZE OF THE
  SQUARE DEPENDS
  ON THE SIZE OF THE
  MOTIF AND YOUR
  TASTE.

PROJECT ONE

A rose-stencilled wall

If you like pattern and have uneven walls, then stencilling is the way to go, as wallpaper requires walls that are smooth and even. This is a very romantic, feminine style for a pretty bedroom. The blue rose-patterned walls have a look of faded textiles and combine well with lace, muslin and plenty of vintage floral fabrics used for cushions and bed covers. The walls provide a perfect backdrop for traditional bedroom furniture like dressing tables, Lloyd Loom chairs, iron bedsteads and wardrobes. Keep a look-out in bric–à–brac shops for pretty old vases, mirrors and lamps that will add authenticity to the look.

Copy this pattern or enlarge it using the grid system. The rose pattern was used here at the size of 60mm/2¹⁄₂in across. The stencil can be cut from waxed card or special stencil plastic available from craft stores.

HOW TO DO IT

Stencilling a wall pattern is quicker than putting up wallpaper and also a lot cheaper. Use the smallest amount of paint on your brush and practise on paper before you tackle the wall.

STEP 1 Make the pattern for the stencil. Coat the back of the pattern with Spraymount and stick it onto the stencil material. Use a sharp craft knife and cut out the stencil carefully.

STEP 2 Peel off the paper pattern, then spray the back of the stencil with Spraymount and leave it to become tacky.

STEP 3 Hang the plumb line 250mm/10in from one corner of the wall and position the card with the line running through two corners. Make a pencil mark at each corner, then move the card down, placing the top point on the lowest mark, and repeat to skirting. Mark up the whole wall in this way.

STEP 4 Position the stencil and smooth it onto the wall. Put the paints on the saucers and dab off brushes with kitchen paper so little remains on the brush.

STEP 5 Begin stencilling with the dark pink in the middle of the rose, then move on to the pale pink for the outer petals. Lift the stencil to check on the result as you go.

STEP 6 Use the green paint for the leaves and stem. Lift the stencil to check the result. Position it on the next mark and repeat the pattern until the wall is covered with roses.

PROJECT TWO
Painting a gingham wall

Gingham is one of the freshest fabrics around and it will never, ever go out of fashion. This project shows how to customise a small foam roller and give the nursery walls a gingham effect. You can do this on a coloured background if you prefer, but white is traditional and always makes a room look bigger and brighter. Most nursery borders look good with gingham, and if you buy one first you can co-ordinate the colours.

Gingham made easy – a simple trick with a small foam roller can transform a nursery wall, making it look bigger and brighter.

HOW TO DO IT

STEP 1 Wrap the masking tape around the middle of the roller, dividing it into three equal parts.

STEP 2 Cut down to the middle of the roller in a straight line following the edge of the tape. Turn the roller and cut all the way around, then once across between the lines.

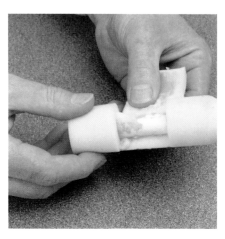

STEP 3 Peel off the masking tape and middle foam section.

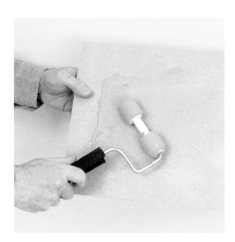

STEP 4 Mix the wallpaper paste following the instructions on the pack, and then mix it half and half with the emulsion paint in the roller tray.

STEP 5 Hang the plumb line from the top of the wall to give you a vertical guide to follow. Run the roller through the paint/wallpaper paste mixture and begin painting in one corner, applying a medium pressure and continuing to within about 5cm/2in of the skirting board. This final bit can be filled in with the offcut from the roller. Continue in this way to complete all the vertical stripes.

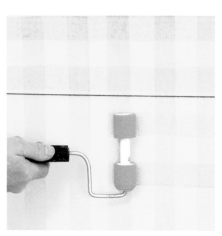

STEP 6 Place the spirit level on the wall and make some small guide marks for the first horizontal band of striping. The next stripes can be aligned with the first, but check with the level on each alternate row so that you don't drift away from the horizontal.

PROJECT THREE

Colour-blocking

The wonderful thing about this decorating idea is that you can use sample pots for all the feature colours. The base colour is applied throughout the whole room, then the dining area is enlivened with blocks of colour. This can be done in all sorts of ways using different colours and textures. A multicoloured wall of squares or rectangles, a graduated colour change from left to right, or deeper, more saturated shades of the background colour are some ideas to try. Contrasts in texture can also be introduced with metallic paints, chalky distempers or by thinning the emulsion paint with wallpaper paste to make a transparent glaze.

The wall of this dining area is decorated in multicoloured rectangles. You could introduce contrasts in texture by using metallic, chalky or even glazed paint.

HOW TO DO IT

STEP 1 Having decided upon the shape, size and position of the squares or rectangles on the wall, mark the verticals along the skirting board in pencil.

STEP 2 Hang the plumb line down the wall as a vertical guide, then use the straight edge and a pencil to make guide marks for the grid going up the wall.

STEP 3 Run tape up from the skirting board in straight lines. Then, using the set square to check that the corners are square, run tape horizontally across the wall, intersecting the verticals and completing the grid.

STEP 4 For a colourwash effect, mix wallpaper paste into emulsion (half and half) and spread the glaze with random brush strokes.

STEP 5 Apply the paints of your choice to the squares or rectangles.

STEP 6 Once the paint has dried, carefully peel off all the masking tape.

TIP
You can use metallic paints as well, to catch the light and make the room appear larger. These are now generally available from DIY stores everywhere.

The African room

YOU WILL NEED:
- PAINT
- MASKING TAPE
- BRUSHES
- DARK WOODSTAIN
- ACCESSORIES SUCH AS WOVEN MATS, DRUMS, BEADWORK, GOURD BOWLS, SOAPSTONE CARVINGS AND HIDE RUGS

The colours of Africa are drawn from the landscape: rusty reds and dark, mud browns of the earth, yellow ochres of the sun, and pale, sky blues are combined with the rich, ebony black of cooking pots on the open fire. The style is plain with organic shapes and bold patterns. Look out for woven and printed African textiles for throws and cushion covers, wood-carved figures, woven grass matting, clay pots, gourd bowls, and African recycled tin and wirework.

This African-style wall reflects the colours of the landscape – the rusty red of the earth, the soft, yellow ochre of the sun, and the blue sky between. A woven grass mat in a bold, spiral pattern completes the effect.

YOU WILL NEED:
- 30CM/12IN X 20CM/8IN RECTANGLE CUT FROM A SHEET OF WAXED STENCIL CARD
- CRAFT KNIFE
- ADHESIVE SPRAY
- LARGE STENCIL BRUSH
- TWO WHITE PLATES
- ABSORBENT KITCHEN PAPER
- PAINT IN TWO CONTRASTING COLOURS (EITHER EMULSION AND VARNISH, OR A PREPARATORY FLOOR PAINT)
- CLEAR, STRONG POLYURETHANE VARNISH (OPTIONAL)
- BRUSH TO APPLY THE VARNISH
- WHITE SPIRIT TO CLEAN THE BRUSH

PROJECT ONE

Stencilling a floor border

Stencilling on the floor is really easy, and you never get the problem of paint running as sometimes happens on walls. For this project you need a 30cm/12in x 20cm/8in rectangle cut out of stencil card. You can then design and cut out your own stencil pattern to form a border around the edge of the room. This could be done on vinyl floor tiles with special vinyl paint, or using an emulsion paint with a varnish to seal it on wood. You could paint a solid background colour, or alternate two colours which can then be reversed for the pattern.

A stencil pattern border can brighten up either a wooden or a vinyl floor. For vinyl, use a special vinyl paint. Use a few repetitive patterns for a balanced, geometric effect.

HOW TO DO IT

Bamboo or cane panels are not expensive but will quite easily transform a room. Before you start this project, paint any areas of the wall that are not going to be covered with bamboo or cane.

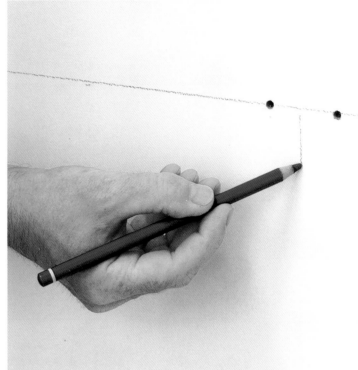

STEP 1 Measure and cut the required lengths of bamboo or cane. Use the fine drill bit to find the positions of the studs in the wall.

STEP 2 Mark the positions on the wall above the height of the panels so they can be found once the panels are in place.

STEP 3 Smooth the panel up against the wall and use a staple gun or panel pins to fix it to the studs in the wall.

STEP 4 Fix the mouldings along the top and bottom of the panels with panel pins and a small hammer.

YOU WILL NEED:

• FABRIC

• 56G/2OZ WADDING

• SCREEN

• SCISSORS

• SPRAY ADHESIVE

• T-PINS

• STAPLE GUN

• BRAID

PROJECT FIVE

Screens

Not surprisingly, screens are enjoying a renewed popularity. They add a regal touch to a room and can hide clutter or divide a room, concealing gym equipment or a home office. Plain wooden or MDF screens, available ready to be painted or covered in your choice of fabric, come with different shaped tops.

Old screens can be found at secondhand shops and if they are scruffy and battered, covering them with a smart fabric will make them look brand new and disguise imperfections. Alternatively, a carpenter could make one to your specifications.

Most fabrics are suitable. Sheer fabrics need to be mounted on a plain, closely woven fabric and treated as one thickness if covering a solid screen. If you wish to use a luxurious but expensive fabric, use it on the side of the screen that faces into a room, with a cheaper coordinating fabric on the other side. Extra fabric will be needed to match printed patterns across the screen.

A screen with frames instead of solid panels can have tension wires strung across and sheer fabric panels suspended between them. Alternatively, lightweight fabric panels can be attached to the top and bottom frame with touch-and-close tape.

If you are re-covering an old screen, remove any old fabric covering and trimmings. Lever out tin tacks: if any are impossible to remove, hammer them into the screen so they do not snag you or the fabric. Separate the screen panels by unscrewing the hinges.

Give careful thought to the positioning of printed fabrics. If the screen is to be stood with one panel more prominent than the others, place the main pattern on the prominent panel. Lay the screen panels side by side flat on the floor and lay the fabric on top. Tuck the edges under the panels. Try different arrangements to see what looks best: centring the design is the obvious choice, but try placing it off-centre as an alternative.

Screens can add a touch of elegance to a room as well as being practical room dividers.

HOW TO DO IT

This screen is slightly padded with wadding on one side, but you could pad both sides if you prefer.

STEP 1 Cut 56g/2oz wadding 25mm/1in larger on all edges than each screen panel. Use a spray adhesive especially recommended for upholstery to stick the wadding to the screen panels. Cut away the excess wadding.

STEP 2 Cut the fabric for each panel front, adding 32mm/1¼in to all edges. Press the fabric and lay the first piece centrally on the panel. Pin to the wadding with T-pins. Fold the fabric smoothly over the side edges. Use a staple gun to fix the fabric in place, working outwards from the centre.

STEP 3 Smooth the fabric along the length of the panel and over the upper and lower edges, folding under the fullness neatly at the corners. Staple in place then trim away the excess fabric just inside the edges of the screen.

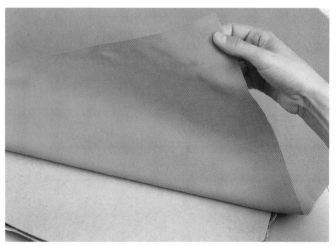

STEP 4 Turn the panel over and cover the other side in the same way, positioning the staples between the first row. Trim away the excess fabric as before. Starting on the lower edge, use fabric glue to stick braid that is the width of the panel on the edges. Cover the remaining panels. Join the panels with hinges.

Window Ways

Windows are quite often a main feature of a room and it is vital to pay them the same attention you would to your selection of furniture and fixtures and fittings. Choice of window covering can set the tone of the whole room, for example, you may select flowing, exotic muslin or tab-topped sheer voile.

You could also decorate the window features, such as the pelmet, in a way that combines your personal taste with the theme of a room decor. In this chapter we look at how you could bring a Romany style to your lounge through the addition of a stylishly painted pelmet that you can make easily from scratch.

We also suggest a way of avoiding the use of curtains or blinds for small bathroom windows. Simply decorate the windowpane itself with etching spray in a way that guarantees both privacy and an attractive window feature in your home.

HOW TO DO IT

STEP 1 Clean the window and allow it to dry. Fold four strips of paper 30mm/1⅛in wide and the width and height of the window into a concertina, then cut out a fancy pattern on one edge. Flatten the strips out and lightly apply adhesive spray to one side.

STEP 2 Fold another three strips of paper into 30mm/1⅛in squares concertina-wise, and draw simple motifs in the middle. Cut these out and spray one side lightly, as above.

STEP 3 Stick the borders around the window up to the desired height, and then arrange the motifs across the window pane in a geometric or random pattern. Mask out the surrounding area with paper to protect from the spray.

STEP 4 Spray on a light and even coating of etching spray. You can always apply a second coat if this is too thin and patchy, but it is best to apply one continuous coat first and then leave it to dry. Peel off one of the motifs to check the effect and apply a second coat of etching spray if necessary.

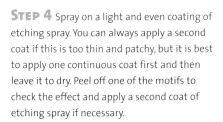

YOU WILL NEED:

- DE-GREASING
  WINDOW CLEANING
  SPRAY AND CLOTH
- ETCHING SPRAY
- MASKING TAPE
- TAPE MEASURE OR
  RULER
- PLAIN PAPER
- ADHESIVE SPRAY

PROJECT FOUR

Decorating a window with etching spray

This gives a cool contemporary look to a bathroom window, and obscures the view from outside. The design is more of a style statement, and the spray could also be used to make a matching border for a bathroom mirror. It is a good idea to make sure you clean the window well and allow it to dry completely before you start.

Decorating a window with etching spray can add a cool, contemporary look to your bathroom. Your own design would do just as well as the one shown.

HOW TO DO IT

STEP 1 Run a frame of masking tape 20mm/^{3}/$_4$in inside the edge of the window, attaching paper to protect the area around.

STEP 2 Enlarge the h$_2$o on a photocopier to fill an A4 sheet, then cut them out and apply adhesive spray to the back. Place the letters inside the masked frame and then frost the window with the etching spray. Peel off the tape and the templates.

PROJECT FIVE
A painted wooden pelmet

A pelmet like this will look best fitted above a medium- to small-sized window. It is really easy to make, being basically a shelf on brackets with a strip of hardboard pinned onto the front and sides.

Pelmets are not very fashionable at the moment but do suit a folksy, traditional room style, and the combination of pelmet and curtains makes a particularly bold Romany-style statement.

One other bonus of making a pelmet is that it creates another shelf in the kitchen and provides a perfect place to display painted plates, jugs or even a vase of flowers.

A hand-painted pelmet sets the tone for a room's decorating style and will be much admired.

The patterns below are the outline shapes for the freehand painting. Either practise by copying them freehand or enlarge the patterns to the desired size and trace their outlines onto the pelmet. Do this by rubbing the back with chalk or using a chalk transfer paper.

HOW TO DO IT

Make a simple pelmet out of MDF or hardboard, paint it black and cover it with colourful Romany patterns.

STEP 1 Mark the pelmet position 50mm/2in above the window recess. Check that it is straight using the spirit level, and draw a pencil line. Mark the screw positions for the shelf brackets on the wall and on the shelf plank.

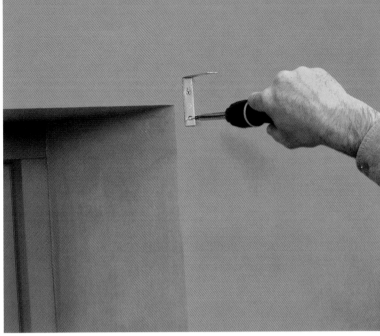

STEP 2 Drill all the necessary holes, insert wall plugs and fix the brackets to the wall.

STEP 3 Cut the end pieces from the length of hardboard, fix to the main length of hardboard and then apply the basecoat. Leave to dry then apply a second coat.

STEP 4 Roughly mark out the pattern with the chalk pencil. Avoid using a ruler – use strips of paper as measuring guides where you need them.

STEP 5 Practise the base patterns on paper first, and when your hand has loosened up move on to paint the pattern details.

STEP 6 Paint as much decoration as you like, then fix the hardboard to the shelf front and sides. Screw the rod fittings into the inside ends. Use a small brush to touch up any pinheads or exposed edges, then fix the pelmet to the brackets.

Furniture Facelifts

Revamping a piece of long-forgotten furniture that you have rediscovered in your loft or jumped on at the flea market is one of the most rewarding aspects of home decorating. Not only will it cost less than buying new furniture, it will provide a satisfying glow as the item is transformed using your decoration skills. These skills can range from simple painting expertise to rudimentary mosaic making. The best part about renovating old pieces of furniture is not giving the items a new lease of life – valuable though that undoubtedly is – but rather the opportunity it gives you to express your creativity and develop your burgeoning home improvement talents.

In this chapter we look at how you can brighten up tables, chairs and headboards using a wide array of materials, including paint, varnish, fabric and even mosaic tiles! Once you have mastered the basic skills you can improvise. Let your imagination go to work.

YOU WILL NEED:

- A PINE TABLE
- A WOODEN KITCHEN CHAIR
- SANDPAPER
- HOUSEHOLD BLEACH
- SCRUBBING BRUSH
- PROTECTIVE GOGGLES
- RUBBER GLOVES
- YELLOW PAINT
- PATTERN FOR CHAIR-BACK DRAWN ON TRANSFER PAPER
- PENCIL
- TUBES OF PALE AND DEEP BLUE PAINT FOR DETAIL (ACRYLIC)
- HOUSEHOLD PAINTBRUSH (50MM/2IN)
- ARTIST'S PAINTBRUSHES (ONE MEDIUM AND ONE FINE)

PROJECT ONE

A painted kitchen table and chair

Preparing meals and eating together form a central part of the Provençal lifestyle, with the kitchen table at the heart of everything. For this project a plain pine table is given a new, more decorative French style with a scrubbed top and painted legs, and the wooden kitchen chair has been given a new coat of bright yellow paint and the finishing touch of a typical French Provençal motif.

Some peeling paint or chipped enamelware is part of this look, and will give the room a sense of history.

Look out for a country-style kitchen chair with a shapely backrest and, if you're very lucky, a rush seat.

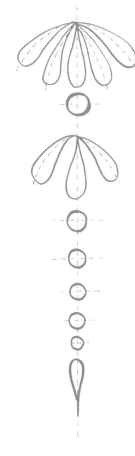

Trace this pattern twice to use across the back of a chair with an extra dot between them. Chalky-backed transfer paper is ideal for this task and can be bought from art shops.

HOW TO DO IT
Give a pine table some character with a scrubbed top and brightly painted legs and paint a wooden chair to match.

STEP 1 Prepare the table legs and the chair for painting by sanding away any loose paint or varnish. Sand the top to remove all traces of varnish, then scrub it thoroughly, first with water, then with a 50/50 solution of bleach and water. Wear goggles and rubber gloves, if necessary.

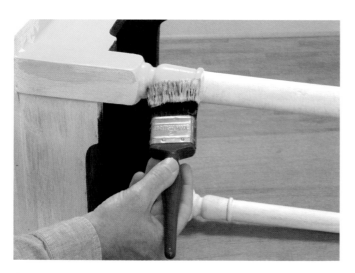

STEP 2 Apply a coat of primer, then two coats of yellow paint to the table legs and top rails.

STEP 3 Prime the chair, then apply two coats of yellow paint. Emulsion is used here for a matt finish, but gloss could be used instead for an easy-clean surface.

STEP 4 Trace the pattern twice to make a symmetrical pattern for the chair-back. Insert transfer paper between pattern and chair.

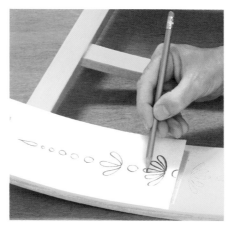

STEP 5 Tape the transfer paper and the pattern onto the chair-back. Go over the pattern in pencil.

STEP 6 Paint the pattern on the chair-back using free-flowing brushstrokes and two different sized brushes.

PROJECT TWO

Rosewood-graining an MDF table top

YOU WILL NEED:

- SHEET OF 25MM/ 1IN MDF
- PVA
- PAINT BRUSH
- DEEP RED-BROWN VINYL SILK AS THE BASE COLOUR
- SMALL FOAM ROLLER AND TRAY
- WATER-BASED CLEAR GLAZE
- TUBE OF BLACK ACRYLIC PAINT TO TINT THE GLAZE (OR BLACK INK)
- 25MM/1IN BRUSH
- RUBBER OR PLASTIC GRAINING ROLLER
- SOFT COTTON CLOTH
- PLASTIC CONTAINER FOR THE GLAZE
- CLEAR MATT VARNISH

Rosewood has a deep red base with a dramatic near-black grain. The real thing is very expensive but it is actually quite easy to fake with the aid of a rubber graining roller. This can be bought in specialist paint stores and even some DIY chainstores. MDF is an ideal material for this treatment because it has a perfectly smooth surface with no grain of its own. Buy a sheet of 25mm/1in MDF cut to a size that will suit your room and the number of people you need to seat, and support it on trestles. If you have never tried woodgraining before, don't be put off, as it is not as technical as it appears. You will need to practise with the graining tool and glaze, however, before you paint the table. You will soon discover the right amount of glaze needed and the technique for rocking the roller as you go.

This rosewood-effect dining table has been made using a sheet of MDF, a rubber graining roller and a deep-red vinyl silk paint.

STEP 6 Spread the adhesive 3mm/ ⅛in deep with a ribbed spreader.

STEP 7 Position the tile pieces in the adhesive.

STEP 8 Once the adhesive has set, grout between the tile pieces.

STEP 9 Polish the mosaic. Paint and varnish the rest of the table.

YOU WILL NEED:

FOR THE STAPLED
   COVER:

• TAPE MEASURE

• FABRIC

• T-PINS

• SCISSORS

• STAPLE GUN

FOR THE SLIP-OVER
   COVER:

• TAPE MEASURE

• FABRIC

• 56G/2OZ WADDING

• LINING MATERIAL

• SCISSORS

• WIDE RIBBON

• TACKS AND PINS

• NEEDLE AND
   THREAD

PROJECT FIVE

Upholstered headboards

Fabric-covered headboards give a neat finishing touch to a bed, and are comfortable to rest against if they are padded. A wooden headboard can be transformed by having a layer of foam glued to the front which is then covered with fabric, which can be stapled to it. Readymade headboards can be covered with your choice of fabric. Alternatively, make a slip-over cover that fastens around the existing headboard with ties at the sides and can be removed for laundering. A row of laced eyelets could be used instead.

Stapling fabric to a headboard can transform the bedroom by adding colour and interest.

HOW TO DO IT: STAPLED COVER

This cover is quick and simple to make so you can transform your headboard in next to no time.

STEP 1 Measure the height, width and depth of the headboard. Cut fabric that is the height plus twice the depth plus 56mm/2¼in by the width plus twice the depth plus 56mm/2¼in. Lay the headboard face up and place the fabric on top, centring any design motifs. Pin the fabric in place with T-pins.

STEP 2 Turn the headboard over and fold the fabric to the underside. Working outwards from the centre on the upper edge and sides, use a staple gun to staple the fabric to the back of the headboard. Neatly fold under any fullness at the curves and corners and staple in place. Staple the fabric to the back of the headboard at the lower edge. If necessary, snip the fabric to lie smoothly around the supports.

HOW TO DO IT: SLIP-OVER COVER

This cover may be easily removed for washing if need be.

STEP 2 Cut four 355mm/14in lengths of 12mm/½in wide seam tape. Pin and tack to the upper and lower edges 215mm/8⅝in) in from the side edges. Pin the fabric right side up on the wadding, smoothing the fabric outwards from the centre.

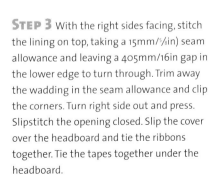

STEP 1 Measure the height, depth and width of the headboard. Cut one rectangle of fabric, 56g/2oz wadding and lining that is twice the height plus the depth plus 38mm/1½in by the width plus the depth plus 38mm/1½in. Cut eight 460mm/18in lengths of 38mm/1½in wide ribbon for the side ties. Tack each ribbon to the side edges 132mm/5¼in and 566mm/22¼in from the lower and upper edges. Cut the extending ends in chevrons.

STEP 3 With the right sides facing, stitch the lining on top, taking a 15mm/⅝in) seam allowance and leaving a 405mm/16in gap in the lower edge to turn through. Trim away the wadding in the seam allowance and clip the corners. Turn right side out and press. Slipstitch the opening closed. Slip the cover over the headboard and tie the ribbons together. Tie the tapes together under the headboard.

What's in Store?

Finding sufficient storage space is one of the major bugbears of the modern home. In this chapter we look at ways of maximising your storage space as well as providing stylish and attractive alternative storage ideas. It is possible to add to a room's decorative theme with clever use of storage space. By removing the doors of a base unit or kitchen cupboard and inserting willow baskets on the shelves as pull-out drawers, for example, you can give a drab kitchen a country look. We also show you how to make a handy kitchen stool that not only acts as a seat but also provides a useful storage box in its base, and explain how you can take an existing free-standing unit and turn it into a tented wardrobe with very little effort, thereby hiding the items formerly on display and creating an appealing feature.

PROJECT ONE

Removing cupboard doors and adding willow baskets

Any base unit or kitchen cupboard can be given a real country look by removing the doors, and using willow baskets on the shelves as pull-out drawers. In fact, it may require a leap of the imagination to convert a standard beige melamine cupboard into something beautiful, but it can be done! All you need do is whip off the doors, fill the holes and pop in the baskets, but a few trimmings will make all the difference.

A melamine cupboard can be painted after suitable priming, and the facing edges of the cupboard can be covered with a wooden moulding. They come in a range of styles, from twisted rope and oak leaves to simple half-moon and square edge. The inside of the cupboard will look good painted in a contrasting colour to the outside, and there is also the option of adding a curtain on a simple net wire. Checked gingham or even linen tea towel curtains look a million times better than old melamine, and they can be tied back to reveal the baskets inside.

Willow baskets as sliding, pull-out shelves transform standard melamine cupboards. Paint the insides and outsides of the cupboard first, and add wooden moulding to the facing edges.

HOW TO DO IT

Simple to fit and a minimalist's
dream, these shelves are magical.
But, as with most tricks, the
explanation is quite simple.

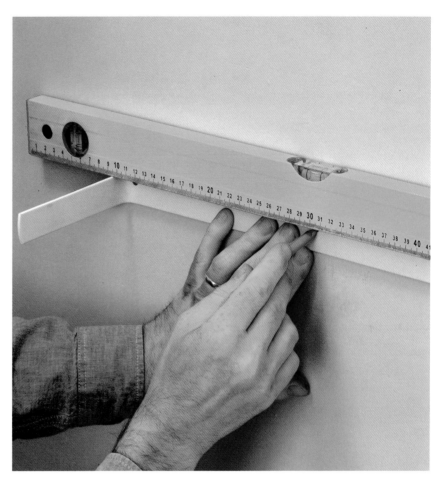

STEP 1 Having decided on the best position
for the shelf, measure and mark it on the wall lightly
in pencil.

STEP 2 Hold the shelf up to the wall and check it
with the spirit level.

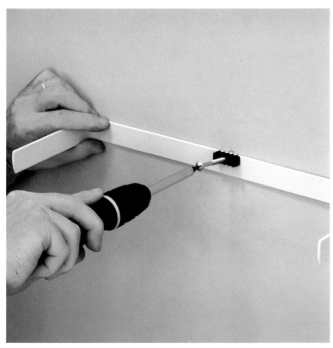

STEP 3 Mark the fixing positions for the supports then remove them
and drill and plug the wall.

STEP 4 Fix the shelf onto the wall supports.

YOU WILL NEED:

• WOODEN STORAGE
  UNIT
• FABRIC
• TAPE MEASURE
• SCISSORS
• 2 BUTTONS
• 2 TOUCH-AND-
  FASTEN DISCS
• GLUE

PROJECT FIVE

Tented wardrobes

Freestanding wooden units are very cheap and are great for storage purposes. The only drawbacks are that they are usually unattractive to look at and everything in them is on display.

You can solve these problems quite easily by making a streamlined fabric cover to hide the unit's contents which rolls up and fastens with buttons to give access inside the unit.

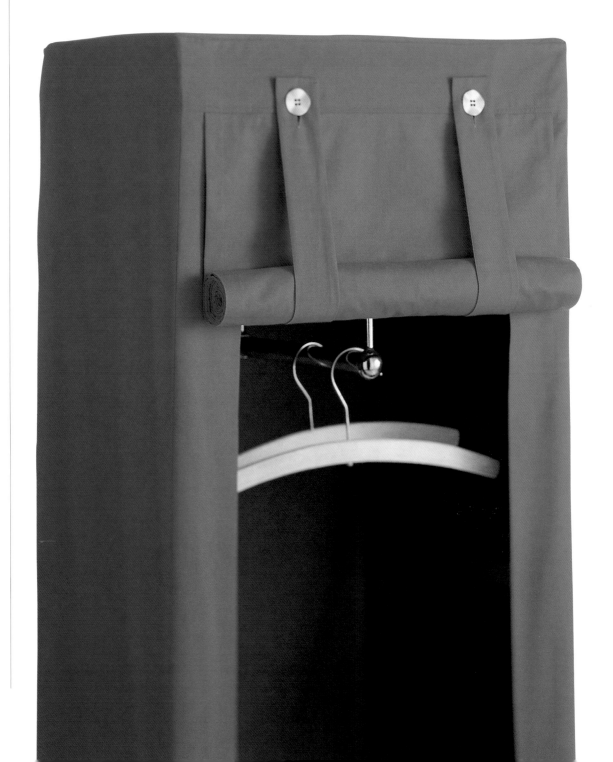

Tented wardrobes are fun and practical. Use the same pattern to cover a wooden bookshelf and hide clutter away from view.

HOW TO DO IT

STEP 1 Measure the width, depth and height of the unit. For the door, cut two rectangles of fabric the height of the unit minus 4cm/1½in by the width of the unit. With right sides facing, stitch together along the sides and lower edge. Clip the corners and turn right side out. Press and pin the upper raw edges together. Take a 15mm/⅝in seam allowance throughout.

STEP 2 Cut two strips of fabric 45 x 12cm/18 x 4¾in for the straps. With right sides facing, fold the straps lengthwise in half and stitch down the long edges and across one end. Clip the corners, turn right side out and press.

STEP 3 Work a buttonhole to fit your buttons 1.5cm/⅝in from the finished ends. Pin and tack each strap to the upper raw edge of the underside of the door 7cm/2¾in in from the side edges.

STEP 4 Cut two strips of fabric for the pediment that are the unit width plus 3cm/1¼in by 10cm/4in. With right sides facing, pin the upper edge of the door centrally to a long edge of one pediment.

STEP 5 For the front borders, cut two 17cm/6¾in wide strips of fabric that are the height of the unit minus 2cm/¾in. Press the borders lengthwise in half with the wrong sides facing. Pin and tack the long raw edges together.

STEP 6 Matching the raw edges, pin the upper border edges borders to the pediment, overlapping the edges of the door. Tack the rest of the pediment on top, sandwiching door, straps and borders. Stitch the upper edge. Turn right side out and press. Tack the raw edges together. Topstitch close to the seam, then 5mm/¼in from the first stitching.

STEP 7 Cut a rectangle of fabric for the sides and back, which is the height of the unit plus 5cm/2in, by the width and twice the depth plus 3cm/1¼in. Join fabric widths if necessary with a flat felled seam. With right sides facing, stitch the front borders and ends of the pediment to the height edges, starting 1.5cm/⅝in below the upper edge. Press the seam open and neaten the edges with a zigzag stitch.

STEP 8 Cut a square/rectangle for the roof that measures the width plus 3cm/1¼in by the depth plus 3cm/1¼in. With right sides facing, pin the roof to the upper edge of the unit cover, matching pediment to width edges. Stitch, pivoting the fabric at the corners.

STEP 9 Turn right side out and slip the cover over the unit. Pin up a double hem. Remove the cover and sew a touch-and-fasten disc to the lower edge inside the front borders. Glue corresponding discs to lower edge of unit. Roll up door. Sew buttons to pediment.

Going Soft

Soft furnishings add texture, colour and home comforts to your living space in the form of curtains, cushions and covers. You can choose fabrics to reflect your personality, such as fun faux fur for cushions or the subtle, sensuousness of sheer fabrics for curtains.

Whatever types you choose, you can use the colours to match in with your general room scheme or to contrast with it. Cushions, particularly, can provide a splash of colour in an otherwise neutrally decorated room. But soft furnishings also have a practical function; for example, floor cushions can help to soften a room's hard edges and provide a comfortable seat. Another sitting-down opportunity is provided by the Cube Seat in this chapter – not only is it practical but it will also provide a talking point in any lounge!

HOW TO DO IT

STEP 1 Cut a 490mm/19¼in square of fabric for the cube top, and four rectangles 500mm/19⅝in for the side panels. With the right sides facing, stitch the side panels together along the long edges, starting 15mm/⅝in below the upper edge. Press the seams open.

STEP 2 With the right sides facing, stitch the sides to the top, matching the seams to the corners. Pivot the fabric at the corners, then clip the corners. Press the seam towards the side panels.

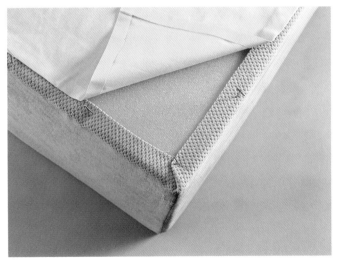

STEP 3 Cut a 470mm/18⅜in square of fabric to cover the base. Press 15mm/⅝in under on the outer edges.

STEP 4 Slip the cover over the foam, positioning the seams at the edges. Pin the raw edges to the base of the foam with upholstery T-pins, folding under the fullness at the corners. Pin the base cover centrally on top. Slipstitch to the base with a double length of thread.

YOU WILL NEED:

- DUPION SILK
- ORGANZA
- AIR-ERASABLE PEN
- SEWING MACHINE OR
  NEEDLE AND THREAD
- IRON
- PINKING SHEARS
- 2 TASSELS

PROJECT THREE

Tasselled table runner

Create an air of sophistication at a dinner party with a silk table runner edged in sparkling organza. A silver tassel sewn to each point emphasises the metallic threads in the organza and hangs elegantly off each end of the table.

TIP
To avoid a noticeable ridge around the edge of the silk caused by pressing, after you have pressed the seam towards the runner, run the tip of the iron around the edge of the runner under the seam allowance.

HOW TO DO IT

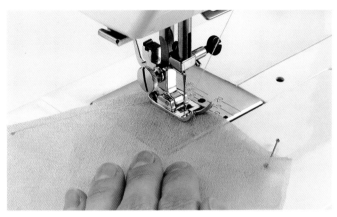

STEP 1 Cut a strip of dupion silk 1077mm x 270mm/42½in x 10⅝in for the runner (allow 10mm/³⁄₈in seam), and cut two strips of organza for the side borders 950 x 140mm/37⅝ x 5½in. Refer to the diagrams to cut the ends to points. Use the pattern to cut four end borders from organza. It would be best to redraw the pattern to actual size.

STEP 2 Trace the two dots onto the end borders with an air-erasable pen. With right sides facing, stitch the end borders together in pairs along the notched ends between the dots. Trim the seam allowance to 6mm/¼in. Clip the corners and press the seams open. Finger-press the seams at the points that are difficult to reach with the tip of the iron.

STEP 3 With the right sides facing, stitch the end borders between the side borders, inside the dots. Clip the corners and press the seams open. Trim the seam allowance to 6mm/¼in. Press the border in half with the wrong sides facing, matching the seams and raw edges. Machine-tack the raw edges together.

STEP 4 With the right sides facing, pin the border to the runner, matching the seams to the corners. Stitch in place, pivoting the stitching at the dots. Neaten the seam with a zigzag stitch or pinking shears, and press the seam toward the runner. Sew a tassel to the pointed tips of the runner.

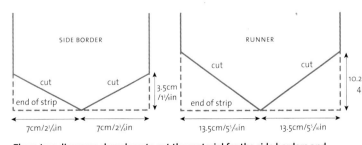

These two diagrams show how to cut the material for the side borders and the runner, as described in Step 1.

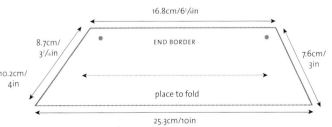

This diagram shows how to cut the material for the four end borders, as described in Step 1.

YOU WILL NEED:

• Toile de Jouy fabric
• plain fabric
• scissors
• thin card pen
• tailor's chalk
• 56g/2oz wadding,
  4m/13ft x 915mm/3ft
• long ruler

PROJECT FOUR
Scalloped quilt

This pretty, scallop-edged quilt is reversible, with a classic Toile de Jouy fabric on one side and a muted plain fabric on the other. The quilt measures 1950mm x 1450mm/6ft 4in x 4ft 9in, and can thus be made from 1525mm/5ft wide fabric.

If you are using a narrower width fabric, join the widths with flat seams, with the full width along the centre and an equal amount at each side. Remember to allow extra fabric to match patterns. Sew the widths together before drawing the scallops.

This quilt is delightfully feminine. Make it the focal point of the bedroom and pick out the colours on the walls and other soft furnishings.

HOW TO DO IT

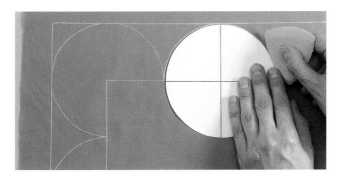

STEP 1 Cut a 120mm/4³/₄in diameter circle of thin card for a template for the scallops. Divide the circle into quarters with a pen. Lay the plain fabric out flat, wrong side face up. With tailor's chalk, draw a 1950mm x 1450mm/6ft 4in x 4ft 9in rectangle on the plain fabric. Draw a 60mm/2³/₈in deep margin inside the rectangle. Place the circle template on one corner, matching the quarter lines to the inner corner of the margin. Draw around three-quarters of the circle on the margin. Repeat on each corner. Move the template along the inner edges of the margin and draw a row of semicircles edge to edge for the scallops.

STEP 2 Cut 4m/13ft of 915mm/3ft wide 56g/2oz wadding widthwise in half. Butt the long edges together and join with a herringbone stitch. Place the printed fabric on top with the right side face up, smoothing the layers outwards from the centre.

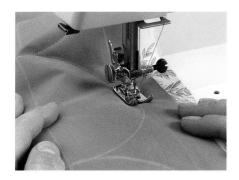

STEP 3 With the right sides facing, place the plain fabric wrong side up on the printed fabric. Smooth the layers outwards from the centre and tack or pin together with curved basting pins. Stitch along the scallops, leaving a 510mm/20in gap to turn.

STEP 4 On the right side of the printed fabric, mark the position of the unstitched scallops with tailor's chalk. Stitch along the drawn lines to secure the wadding to the fabric, taking care not to catch in the plain fabric.

STEP 5 Carefully trim away the wadding in the seam allowance close to the stitching. Trim the seam allowance to 6mm/¹/₄in. Snip the curves and corners. Turn right side out and gently press the edges of the scallops so the wadding is not squashed flat. Turn the raw edges to the inside and slipstitch together.

STEP 6 Tack the layers together or pin with curved basting pins. Lay the quilt out flat, printed side face up. Use a long ruler and tailor's chalk to draw straight lines along the length between the inner corners of the scallops. Starting on a centre line, stitch along the lines with the sewing machine set to a long stitch length.

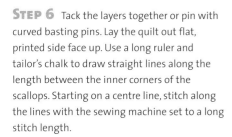

YOU WILL NEED:

- ARTIST'S CANVAS TO SIZE
- DESIGN REFERENCE
- RULER
- SET SQUARE
- PENCIL
- SCISSORS
- COMBINATION SQUARE
- STRAIGHT EDGE
- DOUBLE-SIDED CARPET TAPE
- IRON
- PAINTER'S TAPE
- ACRYLIC PRIME
- 50MM/2IN BRUSH
- NUMBER 6 FLAT BRUSH
- COLOURED EMULSION MATCH POTS
- ROUND ARTIST'S BRUSHES
- MATT VARNISH

PROJECT FIVE

Floor cloth: painting canvas

Hand-painted, individually designed canvas floor coverings owe their origins to the early New World pioneers, who reputedly re-used their boat sails as the raw material.

The design used on this canvas depicts an historical American theme, based on colours and shapes used by native peoples of the South West desert states.

HOW TO DO IT

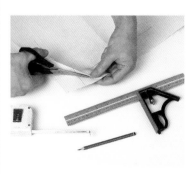

STEP 1 'Square up' the raw canvas, leaving a 50mm/2in border to be folded over, and cut the corners diagonally.

STEP 2 Fold the border to conceal the rough edges, and iron in the crease after damping down the canvas.

STEP 3 Use double-sided carpet tape (available from hardware stores) to secure the folded border permanently in position.

STEP 4 Some canvas is sold pre-primed, some raw. If you buy yours raw, give it a coat of white acrylic primer.

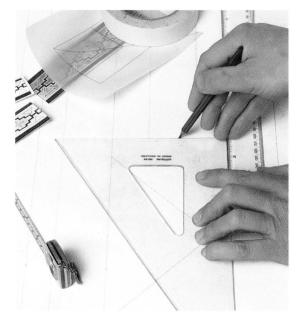

STEP 5 Pencil your geometric design onto the canvas, using set square, measure and straight edge to keep it symmetrical.

STEP 6 Painting: use a number 0 artist's brush to fill in the corners.

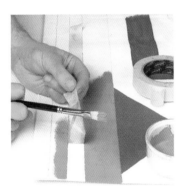

STEP 7 Use masking tape to achieve an accurate, straight side stripe.

STEP 8 Use brown paper to protect the finished areas as you work.

Little Details

Some people would say that it is the smallest details of design in a house that really turn it into a home. In this chapter we explore some smaller projects that could add the finishing touches to a room. First we discover that it is possible to personalise a vase with a simple paint job. Then, basic tiling skills are called for to help you make a mosaic mirror frame in a Moorish style, which you could combine with the Moorish-style lantern also described in the following pages. We show how a basic lampshade and base can be transformed to match in with the theme of a room or to stand out as a particularly attractive feature, using buttons or shells. One of the most important ways of adding personal style to a room is through the display of photographs and we offer a project to make a delightful and stylish padded photo frame. These projects all show that the little things in life can mean a great deal in the world of home decoration.

HOW TO DO IT

Begin by making a simple plywood backing with a wide frame stuck on it as a recess for a mirror. Make the frame the width of three or four layers of tesserae, then you will not need to trim any of the pieces.

STEP 1 Begin by making a simple plywood backing with a wide frame stuck on it as a recess for a mirror. Lay out the pattern before gluing to get the effect you want.

STEP 2 Glue each piece in place . This is a very simple pattern and you should not need to trim any of the pieces.

STEP 3 When the frame pattern is laid, glue the mirror into the middle with a large squiggle of glue.

STEP 4 You may need to cut tiles to fit into the area between the mirror and the surface of the mosaic. Glue uncut tesserae to the outside edge of the frame so that they align with the surface of the mosaic. Grout the mosaic, making sure that the grout fills all the gaps, then polish the tiles and mirror with a soft cloth.

YOU WILL NEED:

• A SELECTION OF
  BUTTONS

• TUBE OF CLEAR GLUE

• LAMPSHADE

PROJECT THREE

Lampshades

It is often difficult to find a lampshade to match the colour scheme of your room but there is no need to worry because lampshades can be painted with ordinary emulsion paint, and a sample pot of colour will be enough to transform two medium-sized shades or one large one. Plain colours look great, but patterns can be stamped or stencilled on, and you can also add trimmings such as a fringe, baubles or beads in contrasting or harmonising colours. The lampshade in the project is embellished with buttons stuck on with clear glue. Before the throwaway culture took over, every home had a button tin and these often turn up at flea markets and charity shops. Old buttons can be really beautiful and even the plain shell or mother-of-pearl types are well worth showing off on a lampshade or cushion cover.

Bases of lamps can be decorated as well as the shades. This seaside-style lamp base has been given a wet sand effect with shells attached using strong glue.